I'm Sorry... I'm Sorry... I'm Sorry . . .

Heartfelt ways to say . . .

I'm Sorry

by
Pauline Locke

Sterling Publishing Co., Inc., New York
A Sterling/Chapelle Book

Heartfelt Ways to Say I'm Sorry

Owner: Jo Packham
Art Design: Pauline Locke
Book Design: Linda Orton
Editorial: Ginger Mikkelsen

Images © 1995 Photodisc, Inc.

Library of Congress Cataloging-in-Publication Data

Locke, Pauline.
    Heartfelt ways to say I'm sorry / by Pauline Locke.
       p.   cm.
    "A Sterling/Chapelle Book"
    ISBN 0-8069-0823-8
    1. Apologizing.   I. Title.
    BF575.A75L63 1997
    158.2--dc21   97-44395
                                    CIP

10 9 8 7 6 5 4 3 2 1

A Sterling/Chapelle Book
Published by Sterling Publishing Company, Inc.
387 Park Avenue South, New York, NY 10016
© 1998 by Chapelle Ltd.
Distributed in Canada by Sterling Publishing
^c/o Canadian Manda Group, One Atlantic Avenue, Suite 105
Toronto, Ontario, Canada M6K 3E7
Distributed in Great Britain and Europe by Cassell PLC
Wellington House, 125 Strand, London WC2R 0BB, England
Distributed in Australia by Capricorn Link (Australia) Pty Ltd.
P.O. Box 6651, Baulkham Hills, Business Centre, NSW 2153, Australia
Printed in Hong Kong

Every effort has been made
to ensure that all of the
information in this book
is accurate.

If you have any questions or
comments please contact:
Chapelle Ltd., Inc.
P.O. Box 9252
Ogden, UT 84409
Phone: (801) 621-2777
FAX: (801) 621-2788

Sterling ISBN 0-8069-0823-8

To my daughters
Katie and Rebecca

But every day I'm growing up
And soon I'll be so tall
That all those little handprints
Will be hard to recall.

Anonymous

I admit my behavior was inexcusable

Joseph Conrad

Life is made up

of so many pieces.

Can't we patch things up?

Please . . .

'Tis
held
that
sorrow
makes
us
wise.

Alfred Lord Tennyson

A Moment of Time

May make us unhappy forever.

John Gay

It is such a secret place — It is such a secret place,

the land of tears.

I'm sorry—I must have lost my way. . . .

Sorry Sorry
Sorry Sor
Sorry Sorry
Sorry Sor
Sorry Sorry
Sorry Sor

SorrySorry

ySorrySor

Sorry

ySorrySor

is always the hardest word to say.

ySorrySor

Across
the fields
I can see

the radiance of your smile and I
know in my heart you are there. But
the anguish I am feeling makes the
distance so very far to cross.

Diedra Sarault

I simply don't know how to say,
"I'm sorry—"

And it isn't the thing

Sun. ~ Margaret Sangster.

At the Setting of the Sun.

you do, dear, it's the thing you leave undone which gives you a bit of heartache

in the dog house

Do you ever make silly mistakes

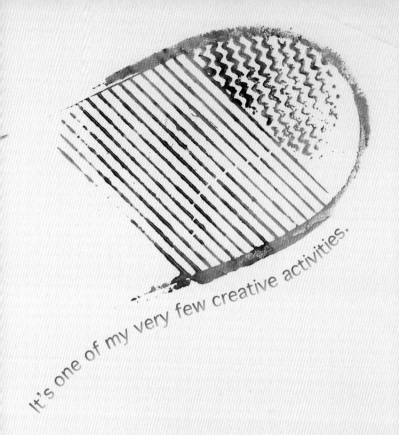

It's one of my very few creative activities.

Len Deighton

Nothing living resembles a straight line
certainly not this journey to and fro,

zigzagging you there and me here
making our own road onward as the snail does.

Marge Piercy

Be still, sad heart!

And cease repining

Behind the clouds

The sun's still shining!

Henry Wadsworth Longfellow

Be still, sad heart!
And cease repining.
Behind the clouds
The sun's still shining!

Henry Wadsworth Longfellow

O! My offense is rank, it smells to heaven.

William Shakespeare

me:: as I am. .Oh, keep me in your heart! But not as your would have

Flora Louise Pousette Dart

Pardon me for being rude.

W_{HY} **IS** it

with SMALL

SEEMS To be

Anonymous

...that such a short

easy phrase...

...and simple words:

I'm sorry,

so difficult

to say?

I was led astray
– I'm sorry

I'm sorry to have been so neglectful—
I really do love you.

Please forgive my imperfections.

Mahatma Ghandi

The weak can never forgive. Forgiveness is the attribute of the strong.

I know now

a closed mouth

gathers no foot

Steve Post

Weeping may endure for a night
but joy comes in the morning.

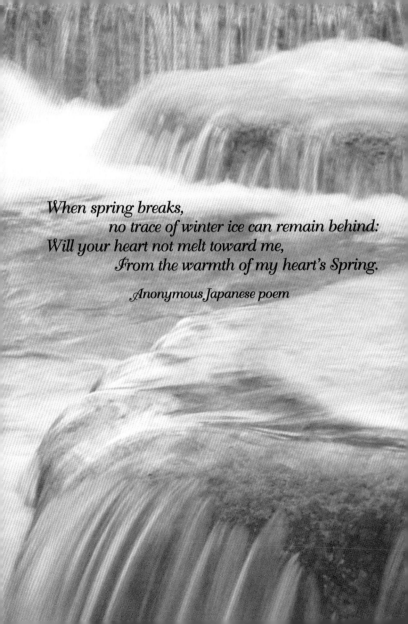

When spring breaks,
　　　　no trace of winter ice can remain behind:
Will your heart not melt toward me,
　　　　From the warmth of my heart's Spring.

Anonymous Japanese poem

To err is human, to forgive divine.

Alexander Pope

Sunday	Monday	Tuesday	Wednesday
		1	2
6	7	8	9
		Marilyn Monroe	
13	14	15	
16	17		19
22	23	24	25
27	28	29	30

I've been on a calendar but never on time.

y	Friday	Saturday	
3	4		
10	11		
26			
31			

JULY

Bad moments,

like good ones

seem to fall together.

Kiss and

Make up?

Let's Bury The **HATC**

Some

things

are

best

when

buried.

Life
is
not
always
what
one
wants
it
to
be,

but
to
make
the
best
of
it
as
it
is,

is
the
only
way
of
being
happy.

Jennie Jerome Churchill

. . . May every loving murmur keep

My smiling image through your dreams appear.

its tender echo vibrant in your ear;

Forgive Me

Adam Mickiewicz

Pauline Locke

And from the formless fantasies of sleep

i'm WORKING ON IT . . . .

SORRY:
repentant
remorseful
CONTRITE
penitent
APOLOGETIC
regretful,

. . . Somehow, it just isn't **enough**

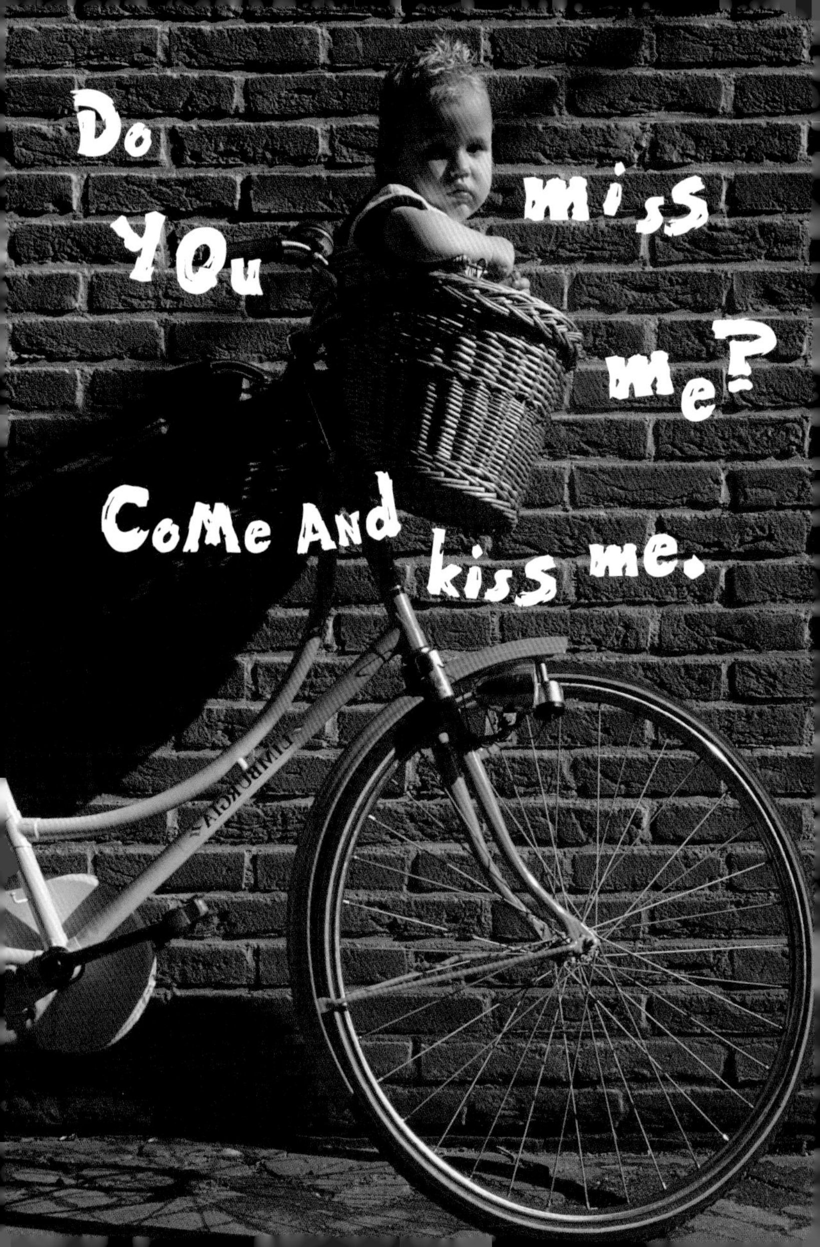
Do YOu miss me?
CoMe And kiss me.

I'm Sorry...I'm Sorry...I'm So